FMG

Faith, Mercy, Grace

BRIANNA HOLMES

FMG: Faith, Mercy, Grace © Copyright 2024 Brianna Holmes

www.faithmercygrace.com

ISBN: 9798327788374

Edited & Formatted by: The Author Queen

Cover Design By: The Author Queen

Manufactured in the United States of America

Follow the Author:

Facebook: Faith Mercy Grace

Instagram: @faith_mercy_grace07

Connect with the publisher:

Facebook: The Author Queen

Instagram: @TheAuthorQueen

Email: hello@thauthorqueen.com

For booking and inquiries:

Email: support@faithmercygrace.com

Dedication

I dedicate this book to anyone who has ever felt like they just didn't belong, battles with their faith, dealing with grief, depression, anxiety, rejection.

I just want to let you know that there is a God that will see you through it all. Put your trust in Him and remember it's not for us to understand the trials and tribulations of life's challenges.

Have faith, and His mercy and grace will guide you. Just stay focused and know that what you're going through or have been through doesn't define you.

Keep pushing; giving up is not an option, and there's always a light at the end of the tunnel. I hope you find in this book motivation and strength to trust that God is always with you, even when you can't see Him.

I hope you enjoy the book.

Thank you for reading.

In Loving Memory of...

Boobie Jean Sparkman,
Randy Shawn Davis Jr.,
Savion Jamal McRae,
and everyone else I've lost along the way.

Foreword

Written by Melissa Lynch

To know Bre is to love Bre.

She writes from the heart. Her poetry speaks to the highs and lows of life with an honesty that resonates deeply in your soul. Inside of "FMG: Faith, Mercy Grace," Bre shares her personal journey, inviting us to join her as she shows us what lies behind her smile.

Through her poems, Bre shows us the real meaning of FMG through the faith, mercy, and grace she found while facing life's challenges head-on. She opens up about her own struggles and the way she overcame. She encourages us to share our own stories and find courage in the midst of storms.

Bre's words reminds us that even in our darkest moments, there is light to be found. Her poetry is a testimony to the power of FMG through difficult times.

As you read this book, I urge you to open your heart to Bre's words. Let them inspire you, comfort you, and remind you that she doesn't look like what she's been through. Thank you, Bre, for sharing your talent with us. Your poetry will touch lives and bring light to the darkest of days.

All my love,
Mel

Preface

Faith, Mercy Grace (FMG) is a look into the experiences that have shaped my life, told through poetry. Growing up in Douglas, GA— many people thought they "knew" me, but let's face it— in reality, nobody really knows "Gay Bre."

This book welcomes you into my world.

Each poem is a piece of my life. I am sharing some of the challenges, the highs, and the lows that have made me who I am today. These poems capture both the hard times and the hopeful ones.

Inside, you'll find my heart on these pages and the lessons I've learned. You'll see that what tried to break me, actually remade me. What the devil meant for my bad, the Most High God used it for my good. And He taught me a whole lot of faith along the way.

FMG is not just about my journey— it's a way of life. It's for you to think about your own life and find comfort in our shared experiences. Because who are we when no one else is watching?

As you read, I hope you feel inspired by FMG to keep going.

Welcome to my story,

Brianna Holmes

A lot of things hurt me
made me feel like I was cursed
when she birth me
after that—
she deserted me
my father raised me while raising hell
only to find out he wasn't even my father
the real one didn't show up
so he was the coward
when he sees my dad
he should salute him
this life I was given really have me clueless
thoughts like I don't want to do this
wishing life had a reset button
remembering as a child I was told I wouldn't be nothing
every other day
it's fighting and cussing
drinking kool-aid without permission
your teeth end up missing
crying myself to sleep
with dying on my mental
I thank God it didn't prosper
when I put that gun to my temple

—rebirth

Cold dark room
no way to escape from my thoughts
face wet—
palms sweaty
phone on do not disturb
sick of speaking and not being heard
if I abandon everyone then I won't get hurt
my guard up
my right hands dead and gone
I've been calling Heaven since they left
God won't answer the phone
so here I am
alone

Do all I can
to be the best I can
still I question if I'm I good enough
did I do or say enough?
or was it too much?
I hate pain so I hate to hurt
but that's all I seem to do
with everything I touch
had to grow up fast
so I be in a rush
life really be tough
thoughts of trying death
but I can't give up
two seeds depending on me
mom making a way
is all they see
physically, mentally, emotionally drained
is what I be
fight, fight, and fight
even when I'm asleep
I get no peace—
demons stay harassing me
pled the blood now leave me be
may not seem like it now
but God chose me
He never said they wouldn't form
but no weapon will prosper against me

—no peace

3

Faith

In a cold dark room
face wet
eyes hurt
feeling drained
worthless
lonely
scared
heart pained from lies and betrayal everywhere
I knocked
doors got slammed
nothing to eat
bottle of water
sip by sip
thoughts of ending it all
hand full of pills
plastic bag over head
breath still in my body

I'm tired

God said 'have faith in Me'
'I'm not just anybody'
picking my head up
I feel lighter
joy in my body
I don't understand it
got a lil' faith now I'm opening doors
for those who slammed it
strong but humble
deep roots planted
like oak trees
with a little faith
you can be
who you are destined to be

Gracelynn—

A love I never got a chance to meet
thoughts of feeling your little feet
smelling your milk breath
and kisses to your cheek
oh how I waited for you to say "TT"
your favorite—
I wanted to be
but God seen you and decided that you were too special
and decided to keep
He gave you wings and a bed made of gold to sleep
play time is all the time with lots of treats
I love you Gracelynn
one day we will meet

Living just to die

Hard to think straight
haunted by past mistakes
can't seem to escape
me, myself, and I
life is what you make it
so I'm the blame for all the tragedy that I'm facing
time don't stop but it's so much time wasted
let's face it
we spend most of our life chasing
just to get it for a split second
then get your life taken
living just to die is crazy

Healer is what I am
not by choice
but God gave me a gift that I just now realized
I was confused of all the broken people I fixed
late night cries for others
my soul bleeds putting peoples pieces together
when pieces of me is scattered
feels like my life doesn't matter
how can I be the light when I'm in the dark?
pained inside still—
my heart
is an enormous size
it was crazy till a few minutes ago
but now I know
I have a spirit of healing
I'm a healer

-Who heals the healer

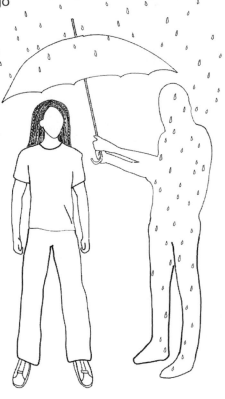

Holding onto my faith
I know God is going to
give me a break soon
and until then
I'll keep fighting for me
others may have left me
but I am worth everything to me
in the end they will see
that greatness is and always has been in me

-Goat

How you view life
and how you live life
most likely isn't the same
is it the way life's meant to be?
or are you the blame?

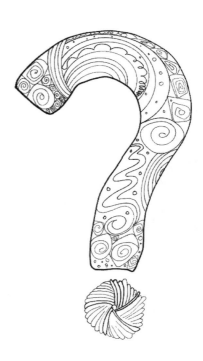

OutKast

I remember the sleepless nights
silent cries
praying that things would be different
never wanted an easy life
just maybe a little gentleness
forced to grow up fast and act hard
heart soft as tissue
loud OutKast so no one would pay attention
to the little girl in me
that screams *'help'*
longing for love
a hug would have broken me down
creating a pond of tears in relief
but all that came was more heartache and pain

I smile to hide the pain
I'm sick of playing sane
lost my nephews—
it was tragic
I feel like I'm the blame
every day is a struggle
they belonged to my sisters
but I felt like I was their mother

—*bleeding*

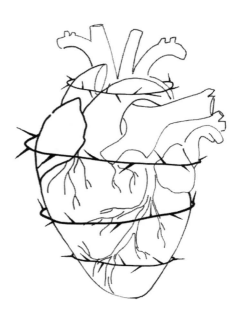

I'm messed up
but I got to make it
this hit hard
I can't shake it
God could have pained my heart—
He really didn't have to break it

fractured

It could have been me in that cell
it could have been me in that cemetery
don't wanna go for bad
it got to be a better way to be legendary
life is scary
it will pull you in that fire
even if you ain't ready
you can do good deeds
but still no recognition
locked up in the house for months
nobody miss you
when you die
everybody wish they could just see you
one last time
reminiscing with all that fake ol' crying
give me my flowers while I'm living
I can't hear you when I'm gone
or take none of them flowers with me
don't even be at my funeral
if you really wasn't rocking with me
I'm tired of the fake love
they be wanting the attention
from you being missing
it's no longer about you
it's about how they feeling

–don't miss me

14

It's going to get worse
before it gets better
the devil want me to take myself off
but instead I keep my head up
better days in the making
I know I can take it
shoulders a lil heavy
can't seem to shake it
mom crying and praying
my sister stressed but won't confess
a lot of food on my plate
a lot of hurt on my chest
thoughts like a casket
the only way I'll get some rest

—a dying breed

Lost

It's said that
life is what you make it
one split second
it can be taken
leaving loved ones shaken
I can't take it
tragedy after tragedy
I've become different
everyone wants me to listen
my heart cold
and my mind on a million
I'm not trying to love
just to be broken
feeling hopeless
bottle after bottle
trying to cope with
pain that keeps growing
easy for them to say
pick your head up
you got to keep going
tears steady flowing
directions—
I don't know where I'm going
jail or hell
at this point
I could care less
head full of evil thoughts
take action without thought
more drama
more problems
forget it
I'm already lost
maybe one day
I'll find my way back
but at what cost?

Judgment

How do you smile with all that pain?
no sunshine in your day
heavy rain
give..give...give
nothing in return
stones steady thrown
at your feet
eyes calm
body at ease
still smiling while you speak
by people you love
scars—
they cut deep
when they cry
you wipe their tears
when they fall
you the crutch
it's not making sense
talked down on neglected sisters
and brothers rejected
but still you kneel
before God
for their protection
excuse me if I'm thinking reckless
pull the trigger on em'
they ungrateful
but when my time comes
I want God to say
'well done— you passed all your tests'

Keep your head up
never let up
situations will have you fed up
faith will carry you through

Life

It's crazy how you're born to die
reading the Bible states to be fruitful and multiply
given mothers, fathers, sisters, brothers, and etc. to love
only to face a day when your world gets shattered
and no dosage of prescription can take the pain away
searching high and low
to find something close
to replace the feeling
of abandonment, fear, and regrets—
it's been 6 years
and you ain't complete yet
time numbs the heart
till one day it hits
like a bullet to the chest
fact still remains
that you loved
just to lose
and the world is a mess

Life is about choices
you can live
or you can just be alive
be wise
for time waits
on no one
and you cannot rewind

Life
takes you
on a ride—
not even a roller coaster
can compare

—all over the place

Living just to die
seems Ludacris—
torture to your loved ones
making some
brain dumb
body numb
I'm just awaiting
for my date to come
it's the only thing promised
at the date of birth
coming into this world
is like a blessing
and a curse

-cursed from birth

Love is always
Overcoming
Very difficult situations
Even if the odds are against you

-what is love?

Nobody wants to die
not everybody
is alive
it's hard
to escape
from the pain
that's buried deep inside

Joke and smile
24/7
to keep from crying
thoughts like dying
got to be easier
but suicide
make you weaker
nobody to turn to
but everybody needs you
full blown sinner
but God wanting you to lead His people
humble but lethal
lucid and paranormal dreams
loud silent screams
wake me up
God

-I can't breath

How can this life be for me?
Got all the answers for others
but none for me
pocket full of money
but
what I want most
ain't got a price tag

-God

I'll give my last breath
for everybody I love
to get what they lost back
eyes open—
still blind to the facts
knowledge will get you hated
loving will get you betrayed

Living in a world
where God gets no glory
but the preacher
gets praised
done seen so much
in this world
if animals start talking
I won't be amazed

—woof

I'm not a charity case
abandoned, beat, and molested
in my life
all took place
9 years old
with no way to escape
prayed to God for my life to take
popped pills
till the pain went away
it was said
I was gone end up on crack
like my moms
one day

-*Pill popper*

I tried it anyway—
but that's another story
for a different day
so many nights
I cried myself to sleep
asking God
why did He give this life to me
full of pain
I was ashamed
like it was my fault
things was did to me
I went to school
and took it out on others
that did nothing to me
I was lost
but now I'm found
I'm a queen
with a crown
my past is not my future
and my present is beautiful
I promised my kids
they will never witness what I went through
what's the use of screaming ten toes down
if you never been through nothing
that made you want to take your feet off the ground?
I'm the definition of holding your head up when you want to hold it
down

–Grace

Nothing
was ever given
my life always
been a mission
had to grow up fast
so I was forced to pay attention
wanted to be a lawyer—
the teacher heard my rap
and got offended
they skipped the suspension
to the streets
they sent me
pregnant at fifteen
man, what does that even mean?

-Shambles

Lights off
baby in my arms
we on the floor
I open a can of peas—
tears drop down my face
I just knew
it had to be a better way
after a few rainy days
God began to put His angels in place
from that day forward
I trusted His grace

-Mercy

Open up
your mind
body
and soul
stop holding back
the potential
to reach your goals
he say
she say
I can't do this
be a trendsetter
who
besides you
knows you better?
you better get it together
don't be out here
dead—
living
because you living a lie
express yourself
we only get one life
waiting on others
is a waste of time
love or hate me
it's all the same
at one point in time

-*Unbound*

The best teacher—

Pain
is something
hard to describe
pain is something
I often hide
pain can be spotted
in the eyes of those
you can't make contact
or the words of a broken soul
pain is a teacher
we can't see
nor hear
nor touch
it just teaches us

Perfect Love

Never giving up
no matter the obstacles
even though
leaving is optional—
fighting not to let go
when times are difficult
being without you is impossible
logical
love for the taken
I love you
and only you—

that's perfect love

Problems

Some things are hard to face at times
it will put you in a heartless place
shut up in the room
just needing space
and time
to bring
peace
to your mind
that never seems to hush
can't be in a rush
move too quickly
you will bite the dust
trying to remain calm
in a world that seems to only want to do you harm
everything you got was earned
knowing how it feels to come from the slums
you filling arms
trying to save people
from a place of heartbreak
you couldn't escape
problem is
they don't see the passion
they just want to take
thinking everyone that got it hard
heart is like yours
was your first mistake
everyone problems ain't your problems
you can't help everyone escape

Sick of taking losses
every time I turn around
I got to close a coffin

—bodies

Smiles
hide a lot of pain
sun shines
briefly in the rain
give a lot for a little of gain
open minded
hoping for a change
fact still remains
over and over
the same thing
thoughts like 'it gotta be me'
start over
go harder
no—
stop
think smarter
who in your corner
giving you sips of water?
in the second round
you win the battle
suddenly
you get the crowd
bells and whistles
you the champ now
get knocked down
all you hear is
boos
now

—a failure

So much on my mind
so much on my plate
hit and run killed my brother
so they say
no charges will be placed
fact still remains
his body
we got to lay
Lord I know I've made mistakes
I asked for forgiveness
so why it got to be this way
my heart getting cold
from all my loved ones who done passed away
they telling me keep the faith
but the bottle
and pills
the only thing that takes the pain away
hard to stay focused
with negativity
always in the way
since I was a jit
I was given the harder way
I know Jesus will make a way
but the struggles
make it hard to pray

–church

Still

I anoint my head
and hit my knees
begging for a better day
it's said that
weeping endure for a night
and joy comes in the morning
I guess my whole life been night
because this rain steady pouring
still—
I stand with a smile
and keep going
heart so big
gifts
it be pouring
so much to give
but nothing comes back
I can count
on one hand
who I know for sure got my back
only the strong survive
and the good die young
I'm sick of hearing that
murders and child molesters
still getting pats on the back
I was 8 years old—
yea
I remember that
what was taken from me
I can't get back
so many attempts to end my own life
because of that
no mother present
as an adolescent
wrong but right
dad present
but I can't remember
one birthday
where I received a present

Wrote an autobiography at twelve
gave it to the counselor
not sure
if she got the message
but she stuck by my side
after she read it
must say
she was a blessing
guess I haven't learned enough
God still giving lessons
had a vision of a white robe
trimmed in gold and
no I wasn't dead
but I was in the pulpit
and the Bible declared
that I shall live
and not die

-*Walking through pain and faith*

41

Stressed out
head grey
being all I can be
just trying to make a way
steady giving
they stay reaching
the Bible says give
and it shall be given back to you
I'm a little confused
the stingy
got it all without worry
the givers hands are dirty
facing hardship
sick of the cards I was dealt
but I can't give up
the little ones watching me

-Make it count

Time

Can't waste it
nor replace it
let's face it—
there's not enough time
in a lifetime
to spend with the ones you love
so the time we have
we must embrace it
putting off today
for tomorrow
is time wasted
if you sleep on time
it will take over your mind

We all die
but do we all live?
stuck in time
like do I belong here?
child to adult
pain runs deeper—
feels like the only way
I can escape
the heartache and pain
is when I'm sleep in my grave

—bury me alive

We are born to live
we live to die
I'm dying to live
and feeling as if
I was born at the wrong time
everyone looks at me
and says
'she strong'
'she's fine'
'here'
'give her some more weight'
'maybe she will break'
little do they know
I have faith
and covered by His mercy and grace
pain is my motivation
so it paves the way
my mind is stronger than my emotions
that's why I'm still alive
today

—overcome

We start life
without a care
open arms
everyone's there
nobody
wants to see you cry
or hurt
from the bottle
to spoon fed
then it's 'take out the trash'
'make your bed'
'I can't stand you'
'get out my house'
nobody checks in to see if you're okay
then comes a call
that you died
now everyone's back in your face
must mean
you're only loved
when you are born
and on your dying day

—Cycle

Where I'm headed
not even I know
when I get there
we both will know

—wandering

Wishing
I could escape the pain
hard to stop the tears
when I think of your name
knowing you're in a better place
I just feel it's too soon
we still had so so much to do
life is just not right
without you

-gone

Woke up
just to wish I didn't—
always got this empty feeling
this world isn't for the weak
got to watch your tone
and what you speak
knowledge will get you hated
if they racist
it's still here
they just hide behind the smiling faces
I can't take it
we need to stand together
and put them in their places

—Colored

Words can't describe how I feel
but I'm glad you lived
so many years
I treasure every moment we had
the tears come and go
some are sad
some are joyful
even though
you and God was ready
it's painful to see you go—
in my heart you will always remain
my lil lady
my baby
my mama
you can never be erased
you told me that you would be there
before the last tear drops
you are the tears
my heart is pained
wings you have gained
I'm thankful for everything
I love you forever mama
now rest

until we meet again 💔💔🖤🖤

—*Eulogy*

-keep the closure

You can't force somebody
to care about you
be loyal nor to be the person
you need them to be—
Sometimes the person
you want most
is the one
you are best without

You got to understand
that some things are meant to happen
but just not meant to be
and some things
are meant to come into your life
but not meant to stay

Don't lose yourself
by trying to fix
what's meant to be broken
you can't get the relationship
you need
from somebody
who's not ready to give it to you

You might not understand "why" now
but I promise you
your future will always bring understanding
of why things didn't work out
So don't put your happiness on hold
for somebody who ain't holding onto you—

Some chapters just have to close without closure....

Yesterday is gone
and tomorrow
isn't promised—
I live every second
free of the world and of myself
giving all that I have to concur my dreams
at any moment
I can leave
I'll make sure that my legacy never dies
after you all say your goodbyes

—legacy, legacy, legacy

You may have called it a suicide
I say it would have been
a peace of mind
I don't think you could have lasted
one month
in this life of mine—
scared
beat
abandoned
molested
mentally abused
all by the age of nine—
fifteen
I didn't want it
but I can't say *rape*
I needed a place to sleep for the night
so I laid there
at the park—
yea
I played and I slept there
stole my clothes
bathe outdoors
got on the bus
and didn't nobody know
they labeled me a bully
but they just didn't know
my soul was bleeding
I had to protect the outer me
by 17
I was counting twenties from stealing
anything to make a living
ruined by men
no mother
so I went to chasing women
long story short
I've never been alive
I just been living

—Gay Bre

'You okay?'
is a question
I hate to be asked
I keep losing my people
so that just seems stupid
tragedy after tragedy
I'm on edge
trying not to lose it
dark thoughts
only if I could get away with it
a lot of faces would be on a shirt—
three of my nephews were taken from me
I'm beyond hurt
just starting their lives
the good die young
will never sit well with me
changed my life forever
heart stay heavy
almost took my life
to visit them in Heaven—
I told God
send for me
because I'm ready
I've been going through pain
my whole life
get it over with already

—bullets

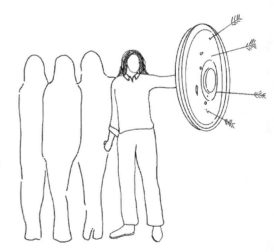

You pray for the sun
I'm praying for rain
we need water to grow
on my knees Lord
send me—
I'll go

I was taught
many are called
but few are chosen
please pick me
Lord
my heart is open

So many trials and tribulations
I don't know which way to go
trying to stay focused on the bigger picture
of the promise land
this world so wicked
it's impossible to live
without sin on a daily basis
I try to be more like you
love and obedience seems so hard to do
when you dealt a hand
impossible to win

I keep getting knocked down
but you always pick me up again
bad thoughts of my past
and present
got me thinking
I ain't worth going to Heaven
still—
I oil my head
and keep on striving
I know you see the best in me
but
I keep fighting myself because
I can't seem to be what you called me to be

So many Christians
looking down on me
so how is it the church where I'm supposed to be?
feel like no one is loving me
is there really hope for me?
give me a sign—
so sick of walking blind
got glasses and I still can't see
physically and spiritually
I'm trying to be all that I can be
got good advice for others
but none for me
since I've been born
I've been given crumbs
abandoned by my moms
mislead by those
who speak in tongues
so I put smoke in my lungs
drank in body
pain
I'm trying to numb
only time I felt wanted
was in a woman's arms
the devil think he won
but God I feel you pulling me
I just can't make the step
cause I'm scared of failing you
I don't think I'm worthy of your presence
It's hard to understand
I'm a sinner but you still keep sending me blessings

Lord— when will I know when I'm ready?
you saved my moms and brought her back to me
I remember as a child
I would pray that if you saved her soul
I'll give you me
it took 20+ years
but you did your part
and I still can't seem to give you all of me
I thank you for not being like man
because you would have been given up on me
Lord
I'm tired of running
this is the night
I take the chance
and give myself away
for Your glory
for Your will
I'll do anything
even if I fall short
I'll never be the same
after being with You
I'm not perfect
and I can't change it all over night
but I give you my word
I'mma try with all my might
I'mma be fighting
to be more like you
until the day You call me home
so if I don't make it to Heaven
the blame is my own
I long to be surrounded by your presence
give me the strength to fight these battles
I can't seem to win
I just heard your voice
they've already won
Lord I want to thank you
for keeping me in your arms
once again

-Surrender

You wanted it
now you got it
so tell me
why you crying?
you spent your last
now you see it wasn't worth buying
grass usually greener
because it's fake
the house or car is cheaper
because it needs more work—
you want the shiny things
but diamonds and gold
can be found in the dirt
took being played and beat
to see your worth
sitting in a lonely house
waiting on an empty spouse
sleepless nights on the couch
bed too big to fill the spot
of what's been lost
I ask is it really better to love and have lost
Than to never have loved at all?

−reality check

I'm ready to be loved
like never before
you know—
the type of love
one would dream of
pray for
even the kind of love
that never dies
in or out of season
love that doesn't revolve around
material reasons
the type that gives you an unexplainable feeling
I want to be in your skin
but let you breathe
kind of love
the
"I miss you already" but
you just walked out the door kind of love...

you know?

What the eyes see
the ears
may be silent to
and vice versa—

you must feel

I have been up all night
seeking to make it make sense
but God declared
it's not for me to understand
just trust His plan
holding on to His unchanging hand
struggling to stay focused
head won't stop
thoughts like
it's time to set it off
too many of mine done
been on a shirt
I'm past hurt
I need 10 of them in a hearse
the way life been going
I feel like I'm cursed

God replied:

stand up my child
someone else has it worse'
I gave you the memories to motivate the strategy
you TT Bre for a reason, but I control the seasons
in due time your light will shine
bringing happiness and peace to many people minds

that's when I heard the song—

"one more day
one more step
I'm preparing you
for myself
and when you can't hear my voice
PLEASE
trust My plan
I am God
and yes I
understand"

A- agree with God
M- move with God
E- end with God
N- never doubt God

About The Author

Brianna Holmes, or just Bre to her friends, is a poet with a knack for turning life's chaos into verses that hit home. Her poetry dives into the good, the bad, and the downright ugly, all while keeping it real and relatable.

Born and raised in Douglas, GA— Bre has seen her fair share of struggles. But through it all, she found her lifelines: Faith, Mercy, and Grace (FMG). These three words are more than just a motto; they're the heartbeat of her poetry. *FMG: Faith, Mercy, Grace* is her story, told through poems that reflect her battles and her victories, and it's a shout-out to anyone dealing with their own struggles.

Bre's writing isn't just about her— it's about everyone who's ever had a rough patch. She opens up, showing that even when things are at their worst, there's still hope. Her poems are a reminder that what doesn't kill us makes us... well, pretty tough.

Outside of poetry, Bre is all about family and community. She pours her heart into giving her kids a better life, filled with love and opportunities she didn't have.

Brianna Holmes is an inspiration with her strong faith, big heart, and graceful spirit. Through her words, she reaches out to others, helping them find their own paths to healing and self-discovery.

Follow Brianna's journey on her website www.faithmercygrace.com and connect with her on social media. For bookings and inquiries, email her at support@faithmercygrace.com.

Ready for the next book?

Did you love this book? If the story captivated you and you couldn't put it down, I'd be incredibly grateful if you could leave a review.

Don't Forget to Leave a Review!

Reviews are the lifeblood for authors. Each one matters immeasurably and helps make my books more visible to other readers who may enjoy them just as much as you did. I pour my heart and soul into crafting these stories, and your honest feedback helps me to keep it up.

Share Your Thoughts on Amazon or Wherever You Purchased This Book

Leaving a review is quick and easy. Simply head over to the retailer where you bought this book (Amazon, Barnes & Noble, Apple Books, etc.) and share your thoughts. Did a particular character resonate with you? Was there a plotline or scene that stayed with you long after you finished reading? I'd love to hear all about your experience!

Thank You from the Bottom of My Heart

Your support means everything to me as an author. With each review, you're not only helping me but also introducing my work to new readers searching for their next great read. I'm forever grateful for you taking the time to leave a review. It's readers like you who make this journey so incredibly rewarding.

Made in the USA
Columbia, SC
08 August 2024